D1824254

CONSUMMATE COACHES

Bill Belichick
and
Jesus Christ

TRACY EMERICK, Ph.D.

BOOKSIDE Press

BOOKSIDE Press

BookSide Press
877-741-8091
www.booksidepress.com
orders@booksidepress.com

Contents

DEDICATION:

To my son, Donny Emerick, and my daughter, Tracey Boies.

Introduction

Think of someone you consider your life coach. Who would it be?

Your life coach is someone who paved the way for you to learn the tricks of life. It could be someone who brought you to your professional success, pushed you when you lost confidence in yourself, someone who believed that you could reach heights. Your life coach is someone who imparted your life's most important lessons – and these lessons you keep as a defense against the many challenges and pains of life.

Simplified, that person inspired you to become the best person you could ever be.

Your life coach does not need to be an inspirational speaker or influencer. He could be your high school mentor, your elementary school teacher, your sibling, a relative, or your parents. Your life coach is someone who taught you important lessons that formed a compass for living your life. Your coach left an indelible mark on your spirit.

Like a game, your coach has trained you to become the best "athlete" as you course through the difficult trails of life. This coach trained you to learn discipline, teamwork, confidence, self-motivation, and all other needed skills to survive and thrive.

According to Encyclopedia Britannica, a coach is one who teaches and trains the members of a sports team and makes decisions about how the team plays during a game. Three noteworthy words: Teach, Train, and Make Decisions.

In the sports arena, a coach's role goes beyond inspiring people. A sports coach is someone who teaches his members tips and tricks to defeat the opposing team. This requires the coach to have ample knowledge and experience to impart something.

1

He holds himself responsible or accountable for the performance, success, or failure of each of his team members.

A coach trains his team members to gain the agility, power, competence, flexibility, and all other innumerable skills needed to achieve the team's goal in a specific sport. Lastly, a coach decides who should play the game and how it should be played. In football, the coach assigns a specific number to each player which determines the football players' positions, based on the players' strengths and abilities.

With that said, a coach should possess three vital skills: Teacher Skills, Trainer Skills, and Decision-Making Skills. We will explore each of them in this book and how these can change our lives.

In this book, it is my goal to dissect the many important definitions and views of a coach and how important it is to have a coach in our lives to guide us through the many obstacles that we face every waking day. Life's a game. Like sports, you should be well-oriented with the rules of the game, the mechanics to achieve it, and the ways to succeed in it.

Like football players, you train to keep the ball close to your goal and strive to shoot it to its goal. Several times, you will fail. But you can't just die trying. You should embrace the reality that no one is born with the gift of achieving that goal alone. So let me emphasize this: *Our life needs a coach to set for us a proper direction and guide us through the tough times. Our coach is someone who will help us navigate through the storms of life.*

In many parts, this book will use the life of two important personalities: Bill Belichick, named America's greatest coach, and Jesus Christ, the man behind the world's biggest religion. Jesus Christ, born over two thousand years ago, was a life coach to 12 disciples. Today, He inspires 2 billion souls across the planet by spreading love and salvation.

Bill Belichick is regarded as the greatest head coach of all time, who made a record for having the most Super Bowl wins in the new millennium as head coach. Today, he inspires many athletes who want to achieve great success in various fields of sports by spreading humility and passion.

The coaching methods of these two people are very much alive today. What makes their coaching strategies similar? How did both achieve greatness? How can we anchor our lives to the various teachings, training, and decision-making skills of Belichick and Jesus Christ, to bring our A-game and become the best players in this complicated game called life?

In this book, we shall identify the various qualities of our consummate coaches and determine the different kinds of coaches to provide us enlightenment in preparation for us to become coaches ourselves.

Keep an open mind and follow along the various stories – old and new – from the life of the man called Jesus to this generation's Bill Belichick, as we parallel their lives to different figures and scenarios and see what it takes to be a consummate coach.

-*Tracy*

Chapter 1

It's All About The Core

Bill Belichick, an American professional football coach who is the head coach and general manager of the New England Patriots of the National Football League (NFL) says this golden quote about being a player:

"Talent sets the floor, character sets the ceiling."

There is no denying it. Belichick, who is named the "greatest coach of all time," knows so well that one may possess great talents and skills, however, by the end of the day, there is one make-or-break element that can transform *great players* to *role models*, *professions* to *lasting legacies, trophies* to *timeless inspiration*, and *achievements* to *transformed lives*. Character sets the ceiling, for without the ceiling, indeed, the floor is without use.

Becoming a coach – like those numerous coaches who brought success to their teams – requires the necessary skills and talents to achieve a goal. A coach needs to have experience, eagerness, an understanding of the sport, and discipline to become qualified at what he does.

While there is much to say about those mentioned elements, this book will not tackle much on those qualifications that make regular, "good" coaches, rather, we will uncover the qualifications – *the character that sets the ceiling* – of a consummate coach. We will study the "extreme coaches" that created not only winning teams in the arena of sports and life but also transformed others' lives, too.

In the introduction of this book, we defined what a coach is. We deduced two phrases vital for us in studying consummate coaches: A coach *teaches, trains, and makes decisions.* Looking at this, we derive that a coach needs to wear three hats on the job: *teaching skills, training skills, and decision-making skills.*

But when we talk about consummate coaches, these are coaches that go above and beyond those three hats. We are going to dive deep into the coaches who left not just a mark on the arena of sports, but they left an indelible mark on the lives of people.

But before that, what defines a coach? Two indispensable aspects represent a "good" coach. I call these the "Two Hs" – the Hand and Head. These are explained below.

The Hand

The first H is the *Hand* – this pertains to the physical skills that make a good coach. This is where the teaching skills and the training skills come into play. This is where the "player" skill of the coach comes in. The *Hand* is vital in coaching. It is the everyday discipline, hard work, sweat, blood, and tears. But it also is about taking responsibility when something goes wrong.

Using building construction as an analogy, the *Hand* represents the construction laborers who use their abilities and strength to build a structure. They build the basic components of a building structure – the foundation, floors, walls, beams, columns, roof, stairs, etc. The *Hand* executes the plan. The *Hand* keeps things intact. Without the *Hand*, everything is just a plan on a blueprint.

The Head

The second H represents the *Head* – the intellectual aspect of a coach. This pertains to the coach's decision-making skills. In a match, the coach will decide which players go first, and which players go last. The coach decides the position of each player and determines their various abilities and competencies. Strengths and weaknesses are balanced properly to keep the team afloat.

Using the building construction analogy, this would be the engineers tasked to design the construction systems, inspect project drawings and designs, manage project schedules and resources, calculate the cost calculations and financial projections, and so on. It takes mental sharpness to keep the project going and to arrive at an output. The *Head* plans, decides, and directs.

"Good" coaches surely possess the two Hs we are talking about. They not only know the tricks on the field as players, but they also know how to strategize to achieve great success.

However, the quote from Bill Belichick at the beginning of this chapter tells us that there is something beyond the aspect of *Hand* and *Head*. Yes, a good coach is skillful, talented, has the capabilities to win a game. He can also have the energy, confidence, and power to advance a team to great heights. But when we talk about "great" consummate coaches, it is not just about these two Hs anymore. Another H comes into the picture.

The last H is what builds the character that sets the ceiling. It's called the Heart.

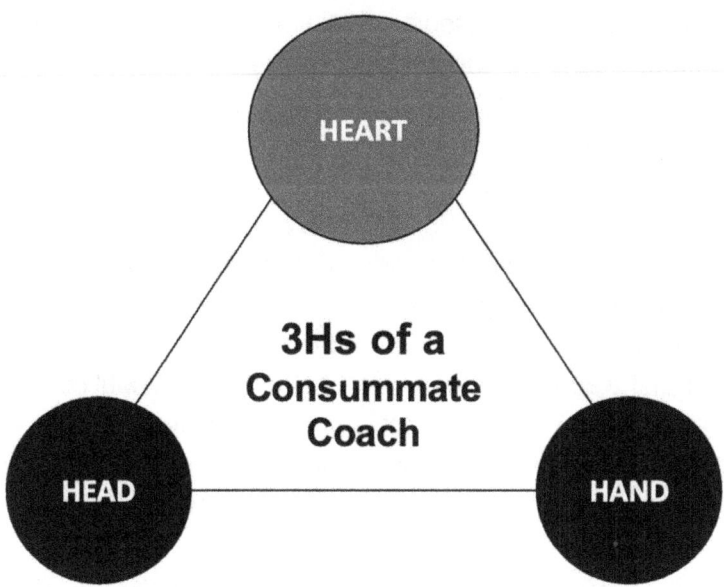

Figure 1. 3Hs Character Combination

Figure 1. A consummate coach has a distinct character of combining the forces of Head, Heart, and Hand. The Heart is located at the center and the topmost portion of the which explains that Heart is positioned to create cohesion between Head and Hand. The Heart binds all the strong aspects of a consummate coach.

The Heart

The Heart, the core of a coach, is what Billy Belichick was trying to explain. It is the heart that builds one's character and motivates and drives people to great success. It is the heart to transforms ordinary players to great ones. It is the heart that makes regular "good" coaches to consummate coaches.

In my other book, *"Extreme Entrepreneurs: Jesus Christ and Steve Jobs"*, I wrote a message about what drives the two extreme entrepreneurs: Jesus Christ and Steve Jobs. One was born 2000 years ago and now has 2 billion believers, while the other one was born in our generation and left a technological legacy for the future. In the chapter entitled "Soul", I explained the commonality of the two personalities. For these two entrepreneurs to leave *a dent in the universe* (as Steve Jobs said), the common main driver for both was this one aspect – *their soul.*

Without the drive of the soul, one cannot determine the exact purpose of an undertaking. In that book, several circumstances prove that both were driven not by money or fame. They were driven by the soul to do great tasks.

Meanwhile, there is an old quote that says, "The mind is the theater of the soul". This means that whatever the soul conceives, the mind reflects it. Both aspects mirror themselves. So, when you are driven by your heart, know that it is what the soul tells you.

When you are driven by your heart, almost everything is possible. We become tireless and weary-less. We become enthusiastic and motivated. We become powerful. This is what great coaches possess, and this is what brought them to the pedestal. But this is not only about the heart for the sport. It is the heart for each person in the team and the drive not only to win the game but to change their lives.

When we are driven by our hearts, we change lives. Our hearts create a direction that motivates our *Hand* and *Head* to pursue and achieve a certain level of perfection. It is the gasoline that pumps the Hand and Head to awaken and be inspired. Without the heart, though, the Hand and Head may still function, but they will not achieve the "consummate" level that we expect from a coach that we try to unpack in this book.

The good truth is, a consummate coach does not really aspire to inspire. Because the heart drives him in coaching his members, inspiration flows naturally without him trying. His character becomes a model for his members, in effect, the members identify themselves with him.

Let's see in the next chapters what characteristics Jesus has as we uncover the question: How did Jesus use his three Hs? What makes a consummate coach?

Chapter 2

The Hand

Now that we learned about the 3Hs' basics, it is imperative that we know the characteristics of a consummate coach through each category. Knowing these would help us determine what sets the consummate coach apart from the regular, good coaches.

The first H is the *Hand* – this pertains to the physical skills that make a great coach. The everyday discipline, hard work, sweat, blood, and tears. Name it. It is the skill of the construction laborers, the sculptors, the welder, the mechanic, the cashier, the bus drivers, all those people whose hands - *literally* - run the operations of a business enterprise on a daily basis.

A consummate coach, however, knows this set of skills much better than anyone else. The Hand is a consummate coach's mantra. It is the *perception into action*. Here in this chapter, let us dissect each of the perspectives of a consummate coach in terms of hard work and dedication to the craft, that makes him a cut above the rest. And by the end of this chapter, let us see for ourselves the meaning of these characteristics of the Hand and teach us golden lessons that will equip us as individuals.

Non-Conformity to Comfort

Many team members think that when they already surpass a certain level of assessment or expertise, things are going to get easy for them. A consummate coach thinks otherwise.

Life, for the consummate coach, is an endless battle fought hard every single day. And it just gets even harder. He does not stop to *conform to comfort.* Coaches have the tendency to treat success differently: when success is achieved, they rest on their laurels and celebrate. There is a certain level of comfort and confidence, a mentality of "we made it, we can do it next time." But this is not how consummate coaches think.

Former WNBA and Olympic Champion Kara Lawson says this in one of her motivational videos at Duke University:

"I was talking with Shay a couple of days ago, and one of the things we talked about was how we all wait in life for things to get easier. Think in your own life if you've waited for something to get easier. [A mindset like] *'Oh I just got to get through this then it will be easy.'* It's what we do. We wait for stuff to get easier. It will never get easier. What happens is you handle hard better."

When we succeed in life, life does not stop. All the more, we are called for greater. The mindset of a consummate coach is to constantly look for more challenges to a point that he becomes uncomfortable in a comfort zone. For a consummate coach, every waking day is a constant quest.

Get Better Every Day

Every day is an opportunity for growth for our consummate coaches. Day in and out, his goal is to *get better.*

In an interview, Basketball star Kobe Bryant was asked about his motivation and philosophy in life. The late basketball icon says, *"I made myself a promise that I was going to work that hard every single day... And that was the most important thing for me – to leave no stone unturned and get better every single day. If I live that way over time, I'd have something that was beautiful. That was my philosophy... if you live your life just to get better every single day, and do that for 20 years... what do you have?"*

A consummate coach has the same mentality: every day is a learning and developing opportunity. Even when the world believes that the consummate coach has reached his full potential, a consummate coach disbelieves it. He does not make limitations on possibilities. There is always, always, room for growth.

The bottom line is: When you think you have achieved your best, think that there is something *greater than the best*. The consummate coach is tireless and never contented; always thirsty for personal and team progress.

The High Standard

A consummate coach's standards and ethics are higher than average coaches. He goes beyond the ordinary by challenging himself to a higher set of standards which explains the perfection of his work.

Dr. Rick Rigsby, an internationally-acclaimed speaker said in his motivational speech, *"To have an extraordinary life, you've got to have an extraordinary psychology. Extraordinary psychology means you got to live in an extraordinary state. To be in an extraordinary state you've got to condition your nervous system, your body, your physiology, [and] your focus, to be at their best. Then to do that though… you can do that! It's not that you can't! We all have the ability. It's because of our standards."*

This statement is true to a description of a consummate coach. A consummate coach believes that to achieve something, you look at a high point of standard. He does not settle for mediocrity. His goals are beyond what others set for themselves.

Figure 2. Consummate Coach Ladder to Success

A powerful quote from our consummate coach Bill Belichick sums up the importance of having a high standard for a team. One of Belichick's famous quotable quote, *"This won't be good enough. It wasn't good enough today. It won't be good enough against anybody else, either"* highlights the importance of setting a high standard daily, otherwise losing is the way forward.

Hard work and Humility

There is a saying that goes, *"Hard work beats talent when talent fails to work hard."* There is much to say about hard work relating to a consummate coach. But a consummate coach does not rely on talent alone. He does the leg work.

There is no one more synonymous with humility than Jesus. From the time of Jesus' birth, He had to hurdle the pains of poverty and walked His way to establish Christianity. He knew He is the Son of God, the Messiah, but Jesus did not have himself born as a King. He was neither born from kings and queens nor was he living in a fancy palace. Think of this. Jesus could've chosen to be born comfortably and live a lavish life. He could have chosen to be born

13

in a place where he can influence others easily. No sweat, right? There is no need of exerting hard work to gain influence.

Instead, He was born from a manger – the poorest possible place one could be born from. He was born in the poor town of Nazareth, a town unknown to the world, out of poor, commoner parents. Nazareth is an inaccessible town surrounded by hills, it did not have enough water supply, thus, there is limited terraced agriculture. With this said, food is not abundant in the area.

Knowing His plight, Jesus knew that He had to work hard for it. Imagine. The magnitude of Christianity's influence today all started from a single worn-out *manger*, a box which cattle and horses eat from. This only shows that Jesus endured the pains of poverty and worked His way to establish the world's most influential religion – with utmost humility.

The Bible exemplified many examples of Jesus' hardwork. John 5:16-18 talks about the Jewish leaders who persecuted Him for working on a Sabbath day. Jesus responded to them by saying, *"My Father is always at His work to this very day, and I too am working."*

If we need inspiration for hard work, think of the consummate coach who was born from a *manger*, and reflect on the hard work he had to endure.

Chapter 3

The Head

As we learned in the previous chapter, the second H represents the *Head* – the intellectual aspect of a coach. This pertains to the coach's decision-making skills.

Decision-making reflects intellect. Before we arrive in a decision, several factors are being considered. A person will sum up all those considerations – weighing pros and cons – and the various aspects in his or her mind before an action takes place. Therefore, decision-making reflects the *Head* of a consummate coach. The mental toughness and sharpness can all be gauged through the decisions a coach made or will make.

Decision-making is vital when coaching – whether it be in a game or life in general. It can make or break a team, a person, or an organization. For example, the coach decides the position of each player and determines their various abilities and competencies before doing so. Positioning the players is a strategy that can spell either success or failure for the group.

The Head requires a good deal of mental sharpness to keep the project going and to arrive at an output. As we learned, the *Head* plans, decides, and directs.

Brent McHugh, CEO of Christar International, best encapsulates the best advice for leaders pertaining to decision-making, written on the website of Forbes.com. I adopted it here with the belief that our consummate coach is best in every aspect written herein:

As a leader, you are faced with a plethora of decisions throughout each day, week, month and year. These choices—big and small alike—may affect those around you or even large networks of people.

Once, as a new leader, I stepped into a meeting that required my team to select a communication platform for our entire network. I hadn't been part of the prior discussions that had led up to this meeting, but I thought I was teed up to make the call. I failed to realize I was making a decision without the right amount of input. Almost 10 years later, the platform I chose continues to be an albatross around my neck. In reflection, I now share what I have learned from others.

There are five keys to decision-making every leader should have in their toolbox:

1. **Information.**

   Take no action until you have gathered the appropriate amount of data. The investment you need to make in looking, listening and learning will vary depending on the potential impact of the decision on others.

2. **Humility.**

   A strong leader makes decisions from a position of genuine humility. You are not the most knowledgeable person in the room on every topic that crosses your desk or lands in your inbox. Taking the issue at hand to a group of "counselors" is a best practice to make sure you see it clearly.

3. **Perspective.**

   Each issue you tackle has multiple layers and a good leader seeks to understand each facet as well as the framework in which the issue exists. Considering factors such as the emotional, historical and cultural contexts is crucial to making the best decisions.

4. **Culture.**

   Fruitful leadership involves creating a culture that is conducive to good decision-making in our rapidly changing world. This requires thinking horizontally on your team and rejecting a top-down decision-making process, as well as having a commitment to lifelong learning.

5. **Plan**.

Having a plan (think a Lean Canvas plan) that is quickly adaptable to current and new realities is a cornerstone to good decision-making. In addition, viable feedback loops will help you hit the target you are aiming for.

Recently I was talking to a colleague about humility in decision-making. He shared how he'd seen a regional director put this key principle into practice when pursuing a new initiative.

This leader would defer to the team member with the most expertise in the skill required to fulfill the goal and then place this "team expert" in charge of the initiative. This, my colleague articulated, was an enduring practice that has benefitted him as he is now the leader for that same region. Remember, you don't always have to be the expert. Others on your team can serve as point people, allowing you and those you lead to benefit from their experience and wisdom.

There are many other things you can do to help you arrive at an effective decision. However, if you focus on these five keys, you are off to a good start.

Belichick, Jesus, and Decision-Making

Bill Belichick as a coach has experienced every single good and bad decisions in life. He says this about decision-making: "We can always look back and second-guess things that were or weren't done, but I'd say really the most important thing for us is to look at future decisions and try to make the best ones that we can."

Bad decisions are part of leadership. We learn and grow from it. Once we learn from it, the learnings will empower us to make the best decisions. For Belichick, he rather makes tough decisions rather that wallow in *"What Ifs"*.

Jesus, meanwhile, also made tough decisions. His decision-making was anchored on His Father's Word. Jesus made all decisions in keeping with the Word of God despite the temptations around

17

Him. Jesus said, "My meat is to do the will of Him that sent me" (as written in John 4:34). By this He meant His food was to obey the Father. This brings us to another characteristic of a consummate coach: a consummate coach does not make decisions by himself but is obedient and concedes to the rules set forth.

Chapter 4

Consummate Coach's Heart

In the previous chapter, we learned that great coaches possess an important characteristic that sets them apart from good coaches. The *Heart* is the added-value driving force that transforms good to great.

But if we talk about consummate coaches, we are referring to coaches that are "greater than great". Great is, in fact, an understatement. According to Oxford Languages, the word *consummate* means *showing a high degree of skill and flair; complete or perfect.* While Dictionary.com defines it *as "complete or perfect; supremely skilled; superb".* Therefore, the requirement that we should be looking at for a consummate coach is perfection in all aspects – in terms of *teaching, training, and decision-making.* Spotless in the aspects of the 3Hs: *Head, Heart, and Hand.*

Other than perfection, consummate coaches also have a unique ability – the ability to unlock the potential of their team members to become coaches, too. Remember this: *Consummate coaches breed consummate coaches.* They are not afraid of sharing their knowledge with the use of their 3Hs, to bring new leaders into the spotlight.

Here in this chapter, let's learn some of the consummate coaches' important values and characteristics as we parallel them to Jesus Christ and some notable people in sports and business.

FIRST: Consummate Coach Needs No Fame

If one is a consummate coach, he will never take a spotlight from anyone because he simply does not need it. Consummate coaches do not need recognition and awards to be acknowledged or revered by people. They are not looking for international fame – instead, they want others to shine.

Studying Jesus as one of our examples, we learn that Jesus did not like fame and fortune. In fact, it is written in Mark 1:43-44 that when he healed a man of leprosy, "Jesus sent him away at once with a strong warning: 'see that you don't tell this to anyone...'"

Instead of being acknowledged for His miracles, he knew that the publicity that the miracles created might hinder His mission to teach about the Word of God, and instead result in people being distracted. Instead of sharing the Word, people will simply marvel at His works of miracles and will eventually lose sight of His core message.

Because of this, Christ had to move His ministry away from the city and into the desert regions. Mark 1:45 (NIV) says, "Instead he went out and began to talk freely, spreading the news. As a result, Jesus could no longer enter a town openly but stayed outside in lonely places. Yet the people still came to him from everywhere.

A consummate coach's *Heart* is focused on the goal and never distracted by popularity or fame. He is laser-focused on a goal that even when fame or fortune comes, the consummate coach never gets blinded by it. While it is true that being a consummate coach would innately pull people's attention, fame never gets into the head of a consummate coach.

Remember, a consummate coach is never swayed by worldly and fleeting desires.

SECOND: A Consummate Coach is Selfless, Never Selfish

Our consummate coach, Bill Belichick says, "Mental toughness is doing the right thing for the team when it's not the best thing for you."

A consummate coach never thinks of his own personal benefit but the benefit of the entire group. In life, a decision may bring a coach discomfort, inconvenience, or disadvantage, but a consummate coach will do what benefits all of its members.

Because a consummate coach does not need fame and fortune, as we learned previously, he is also generous in imparting his skill by teaching others to become consummate coaches, too. He does not hesitate to bring others to the spotlight. He uplifts others even if it means putting him on the sidelines.

Fitness author of the book *Coach to Coach*, Martin Rooney, has a powerful story about selfishness turned selflessness, written in his blog, www.coachinggreatness.com:

There was once a coach in his mid-thirties. He was struggling because his identity was caught between athlete and coach. Since he was still strong and fast, he often challenged himself to either lift more or jump higher than the athletes he was training. He grappled with his fighters and ran against the sprinters. His athlete side still pushed for competition while his coaching side asked for cooperation.

Although the coach was cornering fighters at the UFC and cheering his players from the sidelines of NFL and college games, there was one athlete from another sport who helped him to begin to move from selfish to selfless.

In college, the coach had been a javelin thrower. Although he had won some conference titles, he never felt he reached his potential. When he started training the track athlete to pursue his javelin dream, instead of comparison or envy, the coach began coaching the athlete with compassion and empathy. Rather than looking for something for himself, the coach sought only one thing for the athlete:

To help him surpass the coach in everything he did.

This new coaching mindset inspired him to pour everything into the athlete instead of holding something back. And on the biggest day of the athlete's life, the coach finally learned *the dream of a coach should be to help someone else have a dream come true.*

Why that story is easy to remember because I was that selfish coach."

In this story, we learn that a consummate coach is ready to back off any time, to pave the way for others. He will not hesitate to offer his time, efforts, and talents to develop a new breed of consummate coaches. His *Heart* is offered for others, not for himself. Consummate coaches breed new consummate coaches.

THIRD: A Consummate Coach Takes the Risk for Others

Previously, we learned that a consummate coach is selfless. When one is selfless, generosity flows, always providing for others more than himself. He puts others first, before himself. However, doing this would also mean risks are involved. But like Jesus Christ, a consummate coach does not mind the risks – instead, he embraces them knowing that to achieve the goal, it is a pre-requisite.

However, risk is a double-edged sword. You can achieve successfully or fail miserably. Being a risk-taker is one of the significant characteristics that define the heart of a consummate coach. He is willing to take the brunt of his actions, even the actions of his teammates – always willing to stand for his people and always risking his own. While all coaches have this characteristic, consummate coaches are willing to go toward extreme circumstances of risks.

Elon Musk, a business magnate, Founder, and CEO of SpaceX, the most ambitious space aircraft manufacturer, says that "risk and imagination" were the components of the success of Tesla and SpaceX. No great success was achieved without the element of risk.

Jesus, as a consummate coach, knew the risks involved when he coached his disciples. First, he knew that he will be ridiculed for his selection of his own "team" – composed of fishermen, a tax collector, and some activists. The people wouldn't believe him because of his choice of disciples. Choosing his disciples alone was a risk.

In the Bible, Jesus took the risk for the forgiveness of sins. When Jesus started to preach the gospel, people were mad at him and wanted him to be thrown off the cliff. It is written in Luke 4:29: *They rose up, drove him out of the town, and led him to the brow of the hill on which their town had been built, to hurl him down headlong.*

Preaching was a great risk. His preachings were considered rebellious. The Pharisees at that time thought that Jesus' teachings were not in accordance to their tradition, and so, they did all the means to put His life to end. The persecution, torture, and death on the cross were His ultimate risk.

Bill Belichick is knowledgable of the importance of risk, too. In an article published by NBC News, Bill Belichick exposes how risk is necessary for the sport:

Patriots coach Bill Belichick provided some context for those types of questions before Tuesday's practice when I asked him how he coaches his quaterbacks to balance risk and reward in practice.

Obviously the team wants to get the most it can out of every rep, I assumed, but it also probably doesn't want to encourage bad habits.

As Belichick put it, throwing interceptions in practice is OK because taking risks in practice is OK. Otherwise, how will quarterbacks know what their limitations are -- or the limitations of their teammates -- when they hit the field for a game that matters?

"It's a balance, but certainly I encourage the quarterbacks to take more of a risk in practice than in the game," Belichick said. "That's when a quarterback can really develop confidence in a player, throwing it into a tight spot or having the guy make a tough catch. Can he get it into a small window? You don't want the first time that happens to be in a game and then find out and have him say, 'Well I shouldn't have thrown that.'

"If that's going to happen, let's have it happen in practice if we're going to take that kind of risk. At the same time, we don't want to go out there and throw 12 interceptions every practice either, that's not the idea. But as far as taking a risk, doing something in practice that you wouldn't do in the game, if there's a reason for doing it -- which I'd say there's a lot of reasons for doing that, and we talk about those -- then I'd say there's definitely a place for that."

Not only is that kind of penchant for risk-taking helpful for quarterbacks looking to understand the capabilities of their receivers, but it also helps signal-callers understand when and where a risky throw is worthwhile.

For example, throwing into double-coverage deep down the sideline on third-and-7 from midfield may be a risk worth taking. Throwing into double-coverage for a three-yard gain on first-and-10 from your own 12-yard line may not be.

The situations facing Patriots quarterbacks in practices like Tuesday's are more nuanced, but the point remains: Understanding risk, and sometimes throwing caution to the wind in practice, is an important aspect of quarterback development.

Reflections:

As a coach – *to your team, to your family, or friends* – what are you willing to risk? Are you willing to stand up for your team and your members?

For many of us, we have the tendency to think of ourselves first. Whatever benefits us, or keeps us in harm's way, we choose it. But for a consummate coach, risk is a necessity. But risk should also be calculated. In life, we will be faced with certain levels of risks. Ask yourself, "What do I gain and what do I lose?" before we take a step to risk. We need to accept that the risk may result to failure. We may end up taking the risk and gain nothing. Like what gamblers often do, they risk millions of their investment for a game that may result to them being empty-handed.

But in many levels, risk is healthy. When one practices a growth-mindset, risk is a requisite. A consummate coach believes that he should face the risk otherwise, the goal or target will never be met. It is apparent that in this world, that risk-taking attitude is considered a competitive advantage. The most successful people in any industry takes greater risk than those who are less successful than them.

When a consummate coach takes a risk, it magnifies his selfless love for the members of his team, thereby encouraging everyone to take risks too. When a team learns of this kind of selfless act, it boosts the team's morale, and every single one will gain the strength to face risks together.

Chapter 5

Lessons From Water

Water is the source of life. Without it, we are nothing. Without it, there is nothing.

About 71 percent of the Earth's surface is water-covered, and the oceans hold about 96.5 percent of all of Earth's water. It is the universal solvent. It takes the place of its container. It has cohesive and adhesive properties.

These are a few facts and characteristics of water. I believe that there are water characteristics that are worth discussing here because the nature of water can be perfectly paralleled to our lives. As a source of life, water is connected to our lives more than we know it.

Here in this chapter, I find it best to enumerate the various characteristics of water not only for the appreciation of this precious resource but also for readers to realize that indeed, there are many relatable characteristics that water possesses.

We will also find out that in our quest to find the perfect criteria for a consummate coach, we just need to look at… water. Here's why.

Water Characteristics as it Relates to Consummate Coaches

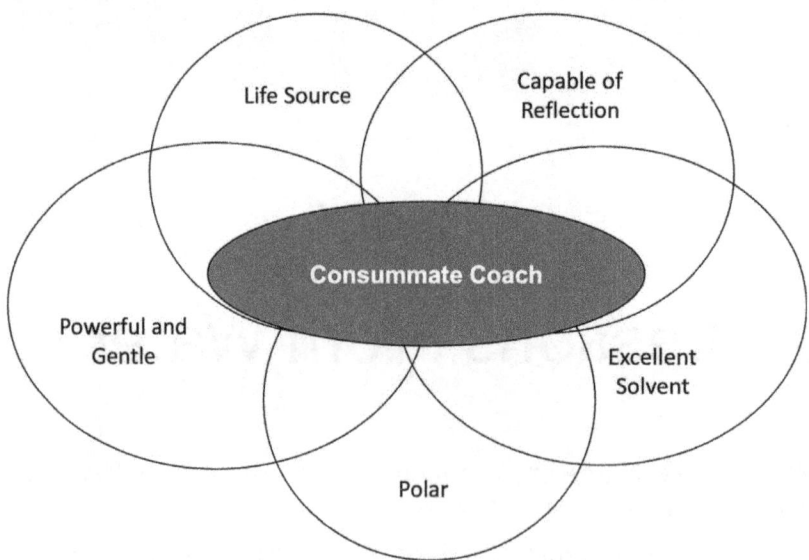

Figure 2. Consummate Coach Characteristics

1. Water is Polar

Water is the only substance that exits as a gas, solid, and liquid state at temperatures found on Earth. The polarity of water is one of the characteristics that we can attribute to a consummate coach. Depending on the temperatures, the water simply adjusts.

Like water's polarity, consummate coaches adjust to varying environments. He plays different roles as a coach. Here's how:

A coach is expected to experience varying situations in life. There will be moments of pressure, doubt, success, fear, betrayal, or persecution. Coaching generally is a combination of bad and good times. But despite these situations, a consummate coach remains rooted in his mission. He adjusts to the varying "climates" and "weather conditions." He adjusts to varying personalities. But at the end of the day, a consummate coach is never swayed by the influence of others. Like water, temperatures can change their form, but at the end of the day, the *water* remains *water*. In the same way, the *consummate coach* remains a *consummate coach*.

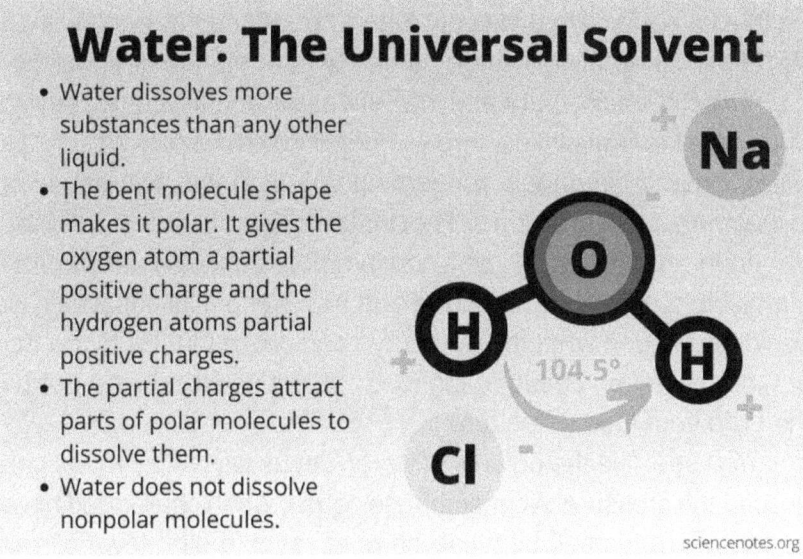

Figure 3: Water, the Universal Solvent (ScienceNotes.org)

Source: https://sciencenotes.org/why-is-water-called-the-universal-solvent/

Like water that changes its form from liquid to solid to gas, a consummate coach can also take in different personas: a coach, a mentor, a leader, an adviser, an analyst, a manager, an engineer, a director, or a producer. Whatever the situation calls, the consummate coach takes a hat.

Jesus, as a consummate coach, also had his share of playing different roles when he lived here on earth. In many biblical stories, Jesus showed his different personas: a son, a teacher, a healer/doctor, a miracle-maker, a preacher, an innovator, a shepherd, a father, a friend, or a sacrificial lamb. He was like water, he was capable of transforming into different forms when the situation calls for it. But He remained as He is - Jesus. Like water, the form changes, but the core remains constant.

Another example was when several temptations came along Jesus' way. As Jesus was fasting, the devil, according to the Bible, sneaked into Jesus' prayer time and tempted him several times. As a human form, he could have been tempted easily. Jesus, as a human form, like all of us, is prone to temptations, fear, or pain. But

He lived a perfect life – the only man who walked this earth without sin. His mission was to spare humanity from eternal destruction.

The Bible says that when the devil came and asked him saying, "If you are the Son of God, throw yourself down. For it is written: 'He will command his angels concerning you, and they will lift you up in their hands, so that you will not strike your foot against a stone.'"

In this story, if Jesus as a consummate coach, wants to prove himself to the devil, or be proud and boastful of His capability, He could have done what the devil says and prove that He is the Son of God; however, Jesus responded: "It is also written, do not put the Lord your God to the test."

You see, like the polarity of water, Jesus was stuck to His core despite the pressure. A consummate coach, when challenged never had to prove himself because he possesses a high level of self-awareness. Like water, a consummate coach can change forms, but the identity is unbent.

2. Water, an Excellent Solvent

Because of water's polarity, with slight positive and negative charges, ionic compounds and polar molecules can readily dissolve in it. Therefore, water is referred to as a solvent – a substance capable of dissolving another substance.

When you put an ionic substance (such as salt) to water, it dissolves to the water. But does water become salt, or the salt becomes water? Of course, water remains as is. However, the salt which has been dissolved transforms into liquid form and becomes part of it.

This is the characteristic of a consummate coach. A consummate coach can influence other people's lives through his "solvency" characteristic, but he does not transform himself or herself to become another person. *A consummate coach knows himself. He does not become his environment, rather the consummate coach influences the environment where he operates.* Instead, the environment is magnetized toward the consummate coach – not the other way around.

Jesus, in this context, was never influenced by his surroundings, neither was His goal blindsided because of the people around Him. Jesus was ultra-focused to his rebellious, non-traditional, and unpopular teachings which, at that time, tore the walls of tradition, causing opposition. But He was an excellent solvent. In the end, because He never wavered in His mission, people adopted His rebellious, non-traditional, unpopular teachings. Now, from 12 disciples to 2.38 billion followers across the globe – a testament of how His influence grew in a span of 2000 years. Christianity is still the most influential and most popular religion in the world forming 31.11% in all beliefs according to Pew Research.

You see, solvency here means influence. The more solvent a consummate coach is, the more influence he has on people.

But the question is, with the power and influence the consummate coach possesses, will this power and influence change the consummate coach? This leads us to the next.

3. Water, Powerful Yet Gentle

The truth is that the power given to the consummate coach does not change him. It should make him become *more of what he already is.* Instead, the consummate coach uses his power to expand his influence and further his goals.

The founder and CEO of messaging app Slack, Stewart Butterfield says, *"It doesn't make you an [expletive]. It just makes you more of who you already were."*

For decades, many people depend on water for power. Its capability of producing electricity through Hydropower is harnessed to benefit people and change lives. Adding to this, it is a form of renewable energy, non-toxic to the environment through Hydropower. In the world, 20% of the electricity source is from hydropower.

You see, in this example, the power vested in water was put to good use. Power did not change water. Water is constantly water.

Jesus has displayed His power and gentleness in many instances. His extreme gentleness is seen in how He cared for the less fortunate. He taught compassion for the poor and needy in Luke 6:20-21 (NIV): "Looking at his disciples, he said: 'Blessed are you who are poor, for yours is the kingdom of God. Blessed are you who hunger now, for you will be satisfied. Blessed are you who weep now, for you will laugh.'"

4. Water, the Life Source

The truth is, a man can survive 1-2 months without food. But without water, a man can only survive for about 3 days. A world without water is… not a world at all, indeed.

Consummate coaches are leaders that bring more than just teaching and mentoring. Like water, consummate coaches provide opportunities for growth, increase the potential of their team, care for their team, giving all that they can for their members.

Figure 3. Natural flowing water from a source

For a consummate coach, power is also an opportunity to duplicate more potential consummate coaches. Like water, it streams from everywhere, it is not self-centered. From the mountains, it flows to streams, rivers, and the sea. When it rains, it is for everyone.

5. Water Provides Reflection

Water is capable of both types of reflection. Still and undisturbed water creates specular reflection, while choppy and moving water creates diffuse reflection.

A consummate coach is one that is still relatable. People see themselves in him. Despite the high standard or the perfect characteristics of a consummate coach, he is being looked up to by others, inspiring everyone to be like him. He is consummate but at the same time, he is not too far up. In fact, he is easy to reach. His members aspire to be just like him. He is a model to his members. Throughout a consummate coach's life, he shows his members that they are capable of greater things.

Another relation to this is how his members identify themselves to the persona of the consummate coach. There is a sense of belongingness, identity, and affiliation.

Who is your coach that you identify yourself with?

6. Accessible to Many, Scarce to Some

Now that we have identified the similarities between a consummate coach to water, we end with one more fact that makes a glaring similarity between water and a consummate coach– that it is *accessible to many but scarce to some.*

Water is a precious resource, and it is an important element in our lives like a consummate coach. However, it is still a fact that many areas in the world still do not have access to it.

In a World Vision article, it says: "If you're among the 9 out of 10 people on the planet who have clean water access close to your home and around the clock, count yourself lucky. Hundreds of millions of people are not so fortunate, and their families pay the price daily. Water-related diseases sap their energy. Carrying buckets of dirty water for hours prevents moms from earning money and kids from attending school. They don't have the water they need to irrigate crops or water livestock. And at the end of the day, it's hard to rest knowing the next day will be the same."

31

World Vision enumerates 10 countries with difficulty in clean water access. Among them is Nigeria, Papua New Guinea, the Democratic Republic of Congo, Chad, Ethiopia, and Somalia, among others.

We liken this to our consummate coach, Jesus Christ. While many countries in the world accept Christianity, there are still many parts of the globe that despise the belief in Jesus Christ. According to the United States Commission on International Religious Freedom's 2020 report, Christians in Burma, China, Eritrea, India, Iran, Nigeria, North Korea, Pakistan, Russia, Saudi Arabia, Syria, and Vietnam are persecuted.

Figure 3 (below): Countries where it is more dangerous to follow Jesus (Source: Christianity Today)

https://www.christianitytoday.com/news/2023/january/christian-persecution-2023-countries-open-doors-watch-list.html

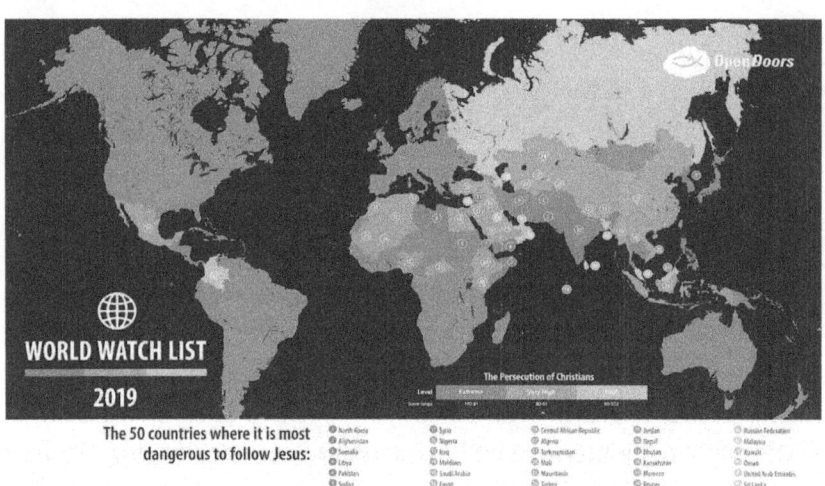

Jordan	Russian Federation
Nepal	Malaysia
Bhutan	Kuwait
Kazakhstan	Oman
Morocco	United Arab Emirates
Brunei	Sri Lanka
Tunisia	Colombia
Qatar	Bangladesh
Mexico	Palestinian Territories
Kenya	Azerbaijan

According to the World Population Review posted on their website: "Religious freedom is not a given in many parts of the world. According to the Pew Research Center, more than 80% of the world's governments interfered with their citizens' religious worship in some way in 2019."

It continues by saying, "Furthermore, although Christianity is the world's largest religion, Christians are in no way immune to persecution. For example, Islamic countries often view other religions as heretical, an affront to Allah, which is considered an extremely serious crime."

we conclude that while there is an abundance of Jesus' teachings in the US, and in many other parts of the globe, it is scarce in other countries that do not exercise the freedom of religion, to a point of declaring it illegal.

I personally believe that like water, Jesus' teachings are meant to be shared and enjoyed by many. Its transformative teachings have brought clarity and transformation to many lives of its followers. So just like water, I make a challenge to all my readers: *Drink that water, enjoy it, but share it with everyone who thirsts!*

Time will come, *just like water,* the world will enjoy the abundance of its transformative benefits.

Reflections:

There are many practical lessons that we can learn from this chapter. But I believe that the most important lesson is simple: The importance of having a consummate coach in our life can be likened to that of water. Our spirit often dries up. A consummate coach should fill us up with its potent energy, its healing power, its guaranteed satisfaction, its life-giving elements, its capability of providing life.

Have you ever experienced being so thirsty? You tried to find water everywhere but there is just none. After hours of thirst feeling, you finally get a bottle of it and realized how valuable that single necessity is for your super thirsty body. After you sipped clean every drop of cold water from the bottle, you make a deep sigh and thanked God for the gift of water.

Often times, especially when we are not thirsty or in need of it, we see less of its value. We see water as trivial when it is abundant. But we come to realize its real value when it is scarce.

It is my hope that as we look for that ultimate consummate coach in our lives, you see the coach's importance as a life source to you – as a great solution, as an excellent solvent, as a gentle yet powerful force in your life that reflects, leading you to inspiration, motivation; filling your spirit with satisfaction.

May that consummate coach be always accessible so that when we meet people who have lost all their hope – people who are spiritually dry, and have given up in life – we are most able to relay the life of our consummate coach to those who are scarce of it. Remember, people will see more of its real value when it is scarce.

Water. Share it.

Chapter 6

Lost Sheep

The parable of the lost sheep is a timeless story that often gets retold when people relate a story about a father's love or God's love to humans. But we can also re-tell this story as it relates to the sacrifice and selflessness of the consummate coach.

If you are unfamiliar with the story, let me encapsulate it. The parable talks about a shepherd with a hundred sheep. One day, he counted his sheep and figured that there was one missing. He looked for that one lost sheep in different places. He was concerned and went out of his way to find that one sheep. When he found the sheep, he rejoiced and threw a feast for it.

To put context at how this story gained popularity, this was how the parable was told: Tax collectors and other notorious sinners often came to listen to Jesus' preaching. This made the Pharisees and teachers of religious law complain that He was associating with such sinful people, even eating with them. This is when Jesus started to narrate the parable by saying, *"If a man has a hundred sheep and one of them gets lost, what would he do?"*, referring to the sinners as the lost sheep.

While this short yet powerful parable can have so many implications in our lives, there are also very important points that we can take up from this parable in relation to a consummate coach.

Before anything else, using the sheep as an analogy is just clever. You see, if there was any animal who is groggy and slow, and often confused about where to go – that's the sheep.

The nature of a sheep is unlike any animal: a sheep always get lost, even when being guarded by a shepherd. All it takes is for one member of the flock to wander off and the rest will follow. Also, another interesting thing about a sheep is that it gets spooked easily. Even of the smallest things you can think of, they are afraid.

We can liken a sheep to a human who is lost and in dire need of guidance in life. How will a consummate coach bring direction to the sheep? And what is the underlying meaning of using a sheep in this famous parable? Here are some of the consummate coach's characteristics as we connect them to the story of the lost sheep:

A Consummate Coach Has a Heart for the Lost

The consummate coach as the shepherd will go out of his way to find that one lost member – even if he could simply let that sheep go, as he has 99 more. Every single person in the group is valuable to a consummate coach. He sees every person as an important contributor to an organization or team.

But for a consummate coach to leave the 99 sheep to find the one lost sheep reflects an even deeper meaning – his love for each member of the pack. Looking back at the nature of a sheep, it just takes one flock to wander off and the rest will follow. The 99 sheep left were in a vulnerable situation at that time.

However, a consummate coach will still take the risk for that one lost sheep. That is the kind of love a consummate coach possesses.

A Consummate Coach Will Save the Lost

Jesus as a consummate coach never fails to exemplify His desire to find the lost. In the texts of the New Testament, *"the lost"* refers to the sinners who have *lost their ways.*

When Jesus was describing His purpose in Luke 19:10 (NKJV), He chose words filled with great wealth and victory for our lives. He said: *"For the Son of Man has come to save that which was lost."*

Jesus' ultimate goal, therefore, was *to save the lost.* It was not only part of the plan. It was the ultimate masterplan! His miracles, His turning of water into wine, the parables He has spoken about, His preaching and teaching, His life and death on the cross – all of those – were for one ultimate goal: *saving the lost.* A consummate coach will do the same: he will go above and beyond his task to bring you back on track.

A beautiful example of a modern-day consummate coach who saved the lost was coach Phil Towel, a therapist and performance enhancement coach. The story was posted on the website www. metalsucks.net:

"For the people growing up in the 90s, Metallica was a great fascination and attracted the respect of millions of fans. However, the band had occasional feuds and it was becoming hard for the members to continue as a single unit.

In the documentary 'Some Kind of Monster', it is finally revealed that the members came to peace because of the efforts and sessions conducted by Phil Towel. He helped the band in staying together for more than a decade."

In this example, a consummate coach does not only find the one who was lost, but he also reconnects the lost altogether. Like the characteristics of water (which we learned in the previous chapter, and which I will add here) he has adhesive and cohesive properties that make *similar substances* or *opposing substances* stick together.

The Role of the Sheep in History

I believe that Jesus used the sheep not only because of the sheep's "*always lost, always afraid*" characteristics. If you look at history, a sheep or a lamb is often used as a sacrifice, even as far as the Old Testament times. You see it as early as the Book of Exodus.

The Passover sacrifice, also known as the Paschal lamb or the Passover lamb, is the sacrifice that the Torah mandates the Israelites to ritually slaughter on the evening of Passover, and eat on the first night of the holiday.

This practice is to celebrate or commemorate the Hebrews' freedom from slavery, or the escape from Egypt, and the "passing over" of the forces of destruction, or the sparing of the firstborn of the Israelites, when the Lord "smote the land of Egypt" on the eve of the Exodus.

In the Book of Exodus, it says, "Tell the whole community of Israel that on the tenth day of this month each man is to take a lamb for his family, one for each household. If any household is too small for a whole lamb, they must share one with their nearest neighbor, having taken into account the number of people there are."

A model of an altar of burnt offering

But one significant role of a sheep is written in Leviticus 4:32-35 which also tells us that the sheep is used as a sacrifice for the forgiveness of sins. It says:

"If someone brings a lamb as their sin offering, they are to bring a female without defect. They are to lay their hand on its head and slaughter it for a sin offering at the place where the burnt offering is slaughtered. Then the priest shall take some of the blood of the sin offering with his finger and put it on the horns of the altar of burnt offering and pour out the rest of the blood at the base of the altar. They shall remove all the fat, just as the fat is removed from the lamb of the fellowship offering, and the priest shall burn it on the altar on top of the food offerings presented to the LORD. In this way the priest will make atonement for them for the sin they have committed, and they will be forgiven."

Notice carefully how the verses here used sheep's blood to represent the blood of sin. The atonement of sin, therefore, is when a sheep is set ablaze on the altar as a burnt offering in the Old Testament.

Now let's learn how this shifted in the advent of Christ.

The Shift of the Sheep

The day Jesus spoke of the parable, however, the concept of the sheep being slaughtered and burned for the forgiveness of sins now stripped off, and gained an entirely new meaning.

When Jesus used the sheep to represent the people who have lost their way (the sinners, tax collectors), and used God to represent the shepherd, He also meant that the penalty for sins, therefore, is for sinners (sheep) to be burned.

But the biggest plot twist came when Jesus spoke of God's mercy in this parable - the shepherd who came looking for the sheep to come home and rejoiced when he found it. The parable shook the old system more than we know it. It now brought a new meaning: that the Lord is a loving God, and that He will find you and will do His best to bring you back home.

Core Message of the Parable

Would the shepherd allow the sheep to be burned when he came looking for it with all his might? Would a shepherd allow the sheep to become a burnt sacrifice if he risked the 99 others for that one lost sheep? Why would a shepherd rejoice when he found that one lost sheep?

In this parable, we figure that the shepherd is motivated and driven by one thing: his heart and his love for each sheep of the flock.

Our conclusion here: A consummate coach is a shepherd who will save his flock, by all means possible. Even if it means being the sacrificial lamb himself, just so his sheep will be spared, he will do so. And this is exactly what Christianity wants to expose in the life of our consummate coach, Jesus Christ.

Jesus acted as the sacrificial lamb because He knew that the death penalty for becoming a lost sheep was death.

According to Romans 6:23, "For the wages of sin is death." But because Jesus, our consummate coach, sacrificed himself as the lamb, the verse now goes on to say:

"...But the gift of God is eternal life in Christ Jesus our Lord."

Parable Reflections

There are many events in our lives that make our situations similar to the lost sheep. When we are lost, as humans, we are challenged by our skills to survive our own turmoil and come out stronger. We are too confident that we can find "our way home", because we are born fighters. We trust our instincts, we trust our intelligence and capabilities. Sometimes we become too proud of ourselves, or overconfident because we have achieved a certain level of success in life, or we received constant praise from people around us. We act like gods sometimes – knowing well what we can do, what our resources have, and what we are capable of. We are wired with sin, that is who we are.

We are genetically wired to think that we are invincible. This is why some people no longer need the guidance of anyone because they feel they can handle whatever life throws at them.

But let me break this up to you: You are not invincible. We often get a feel of our innate vulnerability when we are faced with hurt, fear, uncertainties, and most of all, death.

Like the genetic makeup of a sheep, humans are born with the nature of vulnerability. Yes, we may be at the highest strata of the animal kingdom, the most intelligent of all living things, but we will always be facing situations of helplessness. Yes, my friend. You are helpless. We all are. And like the sheep, we have to be guided by that one single shepherd.

But what if that shepherd cares less about you? How cruel life could be if we have a shepherd who never gets out of his way to find us when we are lost. And when we are at our most vulnerable, we find no shepherd to uplift and comfort us and "bring us home".

The good news, however, is that we have a Shepherd who is willing to find us when we are lost. We may be lost too many times, but He is still going to find us and bring us back to where we belong, guiding us where we should go. He will keep us secured and ready for the next wave of obstacles that will come our way.

In fact, that same Shepherd will risk His life to take you home. You may often commit too many mistakes that make you undeserving to be welcomed back home. But the bright side is, this Shepherd has a heart for the lost, and it pains Him when He abandons you or anyone – and I mean any single one – of His flock.

Our Shepherd has such great love for you. Receive it.

Chapter 7

Bill Belichick:

The Greatest Coach of the New Millennium

In American football, there is no other name that is synonymous with winning than Bill Belichick.

Bill or William Stephen Belichick is nicknamed *"The Greatest Coach of All-Time"* and is the coach behind the most successful team in American football, the New England Patriots. A professional football coach since the 1970s, he is currently the head coach and general manager of the New England Patriots of the National Football League (NFL) considered to be the most successful team in NFL in recent years.

Belichick is also a renowned historian of American football, holding numerous coaching records and gaining six Super Bowl wins as a head coach with the Patriots, and two more championships with New York Giants, which garnered him eight Superbowl wins as head coach and coordinator by far. With these championship belts, Belichick is without a doubt, the greatest head coach of all time and a blazing icon of the sport in the new millennium. His deep understanding of the intricacies of football gained him the name "student of the game" for his knowledge of the ins and outs of football. He is a genius of the sport; with an unparalleled mastery of his *3Hs - Head, Hand, and Heart -* for his chosen career which were elements that elevated him to the highest position.

He is likened to the great shepherd of his flock, and like water, *as explained in the previous chapters*, the world is witness to his

43

gentle yet strong personality. His life is a reflection of his dedication and success, an excellent solvent and a life source to his team. How did he rise to fame?

Belichick's Early Years

Under Belichick's tenure with the Patriots, he was a central figure as the head coach as well as the chief executive during the franchise's dynasty from 2001 to 2019.

New England Patriots 53rd Super Bowl Championship Parade in Boston on Feb. 5, 2019.

But looking back at the life of this man, one can see enormous humility, dedication, thirst for learning and a character that is beyond reproach.

Belichick had his share of humble beginnings. In 1975 in Baltimore, Belichick never had any experience and was not paid much for his work as a coach. But during that year, Belichick amassed great knowledge about the field. He refers to it as a period of "studying".

He took those moments as an opportunity to learn the tricks of the game until he went to Detroit, where he played the Patriots.

Until one day, while analyzing the players' positions, he knew, based on his experience in Baltimore that something had to be done. In an interview with CNBS, Belichick said, "I talked to our offensive coordinator at that time and said *'I know we haven't ever used this formation, but you know, I studied this formation when I was in Baltimore last year. I think this is going to give Patriots a problem. Can we take a look at this?'* We looked at it, used it, and we won."

That was the turning point of Belichick's career. It taught him one valuable lesson. He said, *"Don't be afraid to use a good idea just because it's unconventional or somebody else has not done it. If you believe it's a good idea, then don't be afraid to use it."* When he used his new idea and it worked, that was when Belichick instantly knew of his capability of coaching a league.

That experience kindled an idea that would bring him and his team to the ranks of the NFL. This fired up his thirst for winning. One golden lesson can be learned from this: never be afraid to use a new idea.

But prior to his unparalleled record since 2001, his early career stint was his role as defensive coordinator to the New York Giants head coach Bill Parcells in 1985. Both won two Super Bowls together. Many say that he was close to being remembered as "just the assistant coach who will never make it". But because of his love for the sport, he kept learning, failing, and bouncing back as a better person.

Belichick, Fired

In 1991, finally, Belichick assumed the role of head coach of the Cleveland Browns. 5 years after, on February 15, 1996, however – Belichick had his share of what would appear to be a failure, but came out to be an opportunity that opened wide doors for him. It also appeared to be the most inept decision made by a team that shook the football industry – Belichick was fired by Art Modell, the owner of the franchise. It did not stop Belichick's career, however. Like water, *"the greatest solution"*, Belichick was quick to shift and rise above the challenge of his career.

The firing of Belichick made waves in American football and became a part of unforgettable history.

As noted by SI.com, Belichick was treated *like a punching bag* during his stint in the Cleveland Browns, often portrayed as a grumpy jerk who is clueless about what he was doing – the total opposite of who he is now and what he has achieved in recent history.

After being fired by Modell, it paved the way for him to rejoin Parcells, first in New England where the team lost to Super Bowl XXXI, and later with the New York Jets.

The Rise of New England Patriots

On January 2000, a day after accepting the job as head coach of the Jets, Belichick resigned and accepted a new role: head coaching for the New England Patriots. A fire was set ablaze for the team. The new millennium began with favor on Belichick's side. In the years following that, The Patriots accumulated wins, fame, and fortune with Belichick's life starting to make a sharp turn: Belichick has led the Patriots to 17 AFC East division titles, 13 appearances in the AFC Championship Game, and nine Super Bowl appearances. The Patriots recorded a total of six wins.

The Patriots in Action. BOSTON - OCTOBER 16: Quarterback Tom Brady, No 12, prepares to throw pass at Gillette Stadium, New England Patriots vs. Dallas Cowboys on October 16, 2011 in Foxborough, Boston, MA.

Summing up all of his wins, Belichick has won eight Super Bowl Championships, with runner-up titles four times from his combined time as an assistant and head coach – cementing his name in the hall of fame of NFL and – leaving no room for debate - becoming the greatest coach of all time.

Other than being regarded as the greatest coach, he is also the NFL's longest-tenured active head coach, as well as the first all-time in playoff coaching wins with 31 and third in regular season coaching wins in the NFL with 294.

EAST RUTHERFORD, NJ - NOV 22: New England Patriots head coach Bill Belichick stands on the sidelines against the New York Jets at MetLife Stadium on November 22, 2012 in East Rutherford, New Jersey.

In addition, Belichick is second place for combined regular season and postseason wins, and also the second place for most regular season coaching wins with one franchise. He is one of only three head coaches who have won six NFL titles. Other than this, he was awarded the AP NFL Coach of the Year for 2003, 2007, and 2010 seasons. He was also selected to the NFL 2000s All-Decade Team, NFL 2010s All-Decade Team, as well as the NFL

100th Anniversary All-Time Team, and is the only active head coach on the latter team which even proved more as he sits on his stellar records and trophies.

Belichick, Decision-Making, and New England Patriots

In an Interview with Suzy Welch of CNBC, Belichick says one of the quotes he often reminds his players is *"Every battle is won before it is fought."* Belichick says that winning a game requires a great amount of preparation with the team – that's how a fight is won. It is clear that his coaching method is setting a huge amount of preparation. Belichick underscored preparation when said, "Things happen so quickly. We don't have time for one person to tell everybody what to do. Everybody needs to know what to do in those situations."

When asked how he determines the team's level of preparedness, Belichick says, *"When everybody knows what to do, that's when you know."* Belichick knows that preparation is key to winning, and such takes a great amount of time and perseverance. He says, *"Every battle is won before it's fought. [from] Sun Tzu – Art of War. It's all about preparation. You know what you're doing and you have an idea what the opponent's going to do – what their strengths and weaknesses are."*

One of Belichick's most notable characteristics is his ability to discover the financial potential of people. Belichick is often tagged *"The Chief Economist of Football,"* with the fact that one of his great skills is seeing the financial value of undervalued players. Belichick is known to possess such high financial discipline. In an interview with PBS.Org, Belichick disclosed that he majored in Economics, and there were certain economic concepts that he used in decision-making.

Figure 9. ATLANTA, GEORGIA - FEBRUARY 3, 2019: Tom Brady and the New England Patriots face the Los Angeles Rams in Super Bowl 53 at Mercedes- Benz Stadium in Atlanta, Georgia on February 3, 2019.

It is safe to say that prior to the 21st century, The New England Patriots was generally unsuccessful until the franchise enjoyed a period of dominance with Bill Belichick as its coach.

Belichick's Heart for the Sport

Belichick's father was one of his great inspirations. Belichick has seen and learned the sport from his father, Stephen Nickolas Belichick, also an American football player, coach, and scout. His father played college football at Western Reserve University, now known as Case Western Reserve University, from 1938 to 1940. His father also played in NFL with the Detroit Lions in 1941.

Belichick's heart beats for football. But one important value worth emulating from Belichick is how he centers his motivation. He is vocal about his dislike for material possessions or monetary advantages as an internal motivation. In an interview, Belichick says this about his motivation for the sport:

"None of us got into football to be a professional football player. None of us got into professional football to be a professional coach or manage a cab or team. All of us who got into football got into football because of the game; because we love to go to practice, we'd love to play the game when we were eight, nine, 10 years old."

This statement proves that Belichick's motivation was his heart – it was his love for the sport which drove him every waking day.

His love for the sport can be attributed to his younger years. Belichick always recalls the lessons he learned from his father. Belichick says this when asked about the lessons he learned from his dad: *"Follow your heart. If there's something that you love, and that's your passion when you're young…. do it. Let everything else take care of itself. Don't do it for money or some other motivation."*

On Coaching and "Figuring it Out"

Belichick says that he learned coaching at an early age. From a young age, he analyzes how coaches think, the thought process of coaches, and their decision-making. From there, Belichick learned his own coaching style. However, he exposes that he has learned them from other great coaches as well. He says that he just "figured it out" when he looked at each of the great coaches' styles and mindsets, and he gathered them all and personalized them to work for his own.

"There are a lot of coaching styles… each coach has different personality and styles but for me, determine what works for you. I took a lot [of lessons] from everybody and somehow figured it out. For me, in business or in life, you just have to figure it out."

Belichick Principles of Leadership and Coaching

For our consummate coach, Bill Belichick, his leadership and coaching concept was simple: *"Do your job, be attentive, pay attention to details, and put your team first."* Belichick highlights discipline as the key factor to achieving greatness. "This is what we look at every day when we walk into the building," he says.

He believes that to be successful as an individual player, you need teammates and you better you connect with them. The better a coach connects to his players, or the players connect to each other, the better one becomes successful individually. He also believes in a reward system. He exposes that if one person does something particularly good in the team, everybody receives the benefit.

Belichick is a believer in the importance of strengthening the bond between team members which will connect and enable the team to relax and bond emotionally. The team also does team building, according to Belichick, to bring everything together, but they "take distractions away" such as digital devices like cellular phones.

After every game, Belichick makes it a habit to check the errors that are made by the coaching staff. He believes that coaching is vital in any game as "good players cannot overcome bad coaching." Belichick had this coaching principle: "Some players process some things easier and quicker than others do, and then others process things easier and quicker than another player. You just have to find that balance with each player regardless of what year he's in or what position he plays. That's just coaching."

Chapter 8

Jesus Christ:

The Servant Consummate Coach

Jesus Christ was born more than 2000 years ago. What started to be a story of a man who made miracles and shared parables concluded in a gruesome death. Fast-forward to today, He now amassed two billion followers across the globe. The biggest religion of all time. The most influential person who has ever walked this planet. The most popular name of all ages. Honored. Revered. Worshipped.

But contradicting what others think about Jesus, He was not born in a palace of kings. In fact, His humble beginnings were *beyond humble*: born from a manger, from poor and lowly parents, in a town unknown to the world. Knowing his background, one would have considered him an outcast. Unknown. Ordinary. Unsuccessful. Unremarkable. Loser.

But his coaching or leadership style had a different element that is considered among the best, worthy of emulation. His style goes beyond the mastery of His 3Hs (Head, Hand, and Heart). In this chapter let us study with open minds and hearts why and how Jesus elevated to a superstar status, a symbol of the biggest religion in the world, and believed by Christians as the "King of kings and Lord of lords".

Before we continue, let me set the record straight for people who think that Jesus only rose to fame because of His unique way of death - the crucifixion. No. We have to remember that history speaks of *not only one, not two, not three crucified* people in the past. Roman Crucifixion was imposed on thousands and thousands of people during Christ's time. According to LiveScience.com, in antiquity, tens and thousands of people were crucified, which at the time was considered to be one of the most brutal and shameful ways to die.

Jesus' Coaching Beginnings

If we look at how Jesus rose to fame, it cannot be attributed alone to His gruesome way of death. Much of it is attributed, however, to His teachings which brought a different vision and direction to the world. He coached 12 disciples to spread these teachings, mastered His 3Hs in the process, and in addition, involved two other important elements that elevated Him to becoming the ultimate leader and coach: *eternity and spirit.*

Figure 10. The Jesus Sends Out His Disciples lithography by artist Scheuchl 1907 in the book "Zivot Jezisa Krista bozskeho Spasitela naseho" printed in Trnava.

Jesus started discipleship or coaching at the age of 30, with only 12 disciples. Unlike a football team, there were no defensive or offensive strategies. Jesus Christ's rule was simple: spread the good news of *love, spirit, and eternity*. Like a shepherd to His flock, He anchored His teachings solely on love, and concern for the less fortunate, for the sick, and for the sinners.

His message of love – His very core message – is one of the elements that drove Him from start to end. But Jesus' leadership style was a standout. When the Bible said, "His ways are not our ways," looking at His leadership, indeed, His methods were different and were executed differently. In fact, His ways were contradictory to the leadership styles of the past and our generation at present. Here's why.

Jesus' Servant-Leadership Style

Figure 11. Jesus washes the feet of Peter, fresco in the church of Saint Matthew in Stitar, Croatia.

Jesus' leadership method is the exact opposite of the way leaders nowadays lead. While most leaders are driven by *"on top of the game", "I am the best," and "I will stay on top"* mentality, these were not the idea of leadership for Jesus. His type of leadership was not aimed at controlling people or being autocratic, or coercive. Jesus' leadership style was centered and founded on *servant-leadership.*

In servant-leadership, Jesus taught that to be a leader, you must also be a servant. This was magnified when Jesus washed the feet of His own disciples.

On the website MindaNews.com, it says *"Jesus' washing of the feet is a symbolic act to dramatize His view of leadership – humble and loving service. This should be the underlying motivation in the exercise of leadership. Jesus presents Himself as the model and asks His disciples to follow His example.*

Generally, leadership is often regarded as a high position where the *servants follow* and *leaders demand.* Leaders are often regarded as kings and lords by some, but Jesus tore down this culture and brought a new and refreshing meaning to leadership for everyone to follow – *to be a servant.* Jesus' leadership, therefore, is one that shows humility, respect, and love, contradictory to the usual power, might, fame, and force.

Jesus Speaks of What Matters Most: Eternity

If we talk of a specific coaching experience of Jesus, we can look at the Book of Luke 10:1-12 as it narrates how Jesus coached 70 people to spread the good news. I summarized them below:

Jesus appointed seventy-two others and sent them *two by two* ahead of him to every town and place where he was about to go. He told the 70 people, "The harvest is plentiful, but the workers are few. Ask the Lord of the harvest, therefore, to send out workers into his harvest field. Go! I am sending you out like lambs among wolves. Do not take a purse or bag or sandals; and do not greet anyone on the road."

Jesus had a rule for the disciples. Like a coach, he also laid out the masterplan and the intricacy of things that had to be done, step by step.

When one enters a house, Jesus instructed them to first say, *"Peace to this house."* If someone, according to Jesus, who promotes peace is there, your peace will rest on them; if not, it will return to you. Among the other rules were: "Stay there, eating and drinking whatever they give you, for the worker deserves his wages. Do not move around from house to house."

Jesus also went on to say, "When you enter a town and are welcomed, eat what is offered to you. Heal the sick who are there and tell them, *'The kingdom of God has come near to you.'* But when you enter a town and are not welcomed, go into its streets and say, 'Even the dust of your town we wipe from our feet as a warning to you. Yet be sure of this: The kingdom of God has come near. I tell you, it will be more bearable on that day for Sodom than for that town.'"

Leadership: Giving Affirmation

Jesus had a beautiful approach to coaching his 70 disciples. Mark D. Roberts wrote this in his article posted on the Fuller Du Pree Center for Leadership website that sums up the beauty of Jesus' coaching style:

Luke does not describe what happened when the seventy went out to do what Jesus has given to them. We do, however, get a snippet of their report to Jesus when they returned from their mission trip. "Lord," they said, "in your name, even the demons submit to us!" (Luke 10:17).

Jesus's response to these disciples is not what we might expect. No "Great job" or high five. Rather, Jesus said, "I watched Satan fall from heaven like a flash of lightning. See, I have given you authority to tread on snakes and scorpions, and over all the power of the enemy, and nothing will hurt you. Nevertheless, do not rejoice at this, that the spirits submit to you, but rejoice that your names are written in heaven" (Luke 10:18-20).

When we unpack this odd saying of Jesus, we see him in the role of a coach. At first, he speaks words of affirmation. When his disciples were exercising authority over demons, Jesus "saw" the defeat of Satan. He could sense in his spirit that Satan's kingdom was coming to an end as his followers vanquished Satan's minions. It was as if Jesus was saying, "What you experienced was actually far more than demons submitting to you. This was evidence of the eternal downfall of Satan." That's a pretty strong affirmation if you ask me.

Yet Jesus didn't just affirm His disciples. He also corrected and redirected them. Yes, the spirits were subject to their authority. But far more important than this was the fact that the names of the disciples were "written in heaven" (Luke 10:20). This meant more than just the salvation of their souls. Having their names in the Book of Life signified a permanent relationship with God. And this, Jesus said, is a fantastic reason to rejoice.

When I consider the affirmation and the correction offered by Jesus as a coach, I'm impressed by what He urges his disciples to value most of all. Beyond performance, even impressive demonstrations of spiritual power, relationship matters most. That's not to say we shouldn't be pleased when we are able to serve the Lord in tangible ways. But in our performance-driven society, we can easily let what we do for God matter more than our relationship with God. Jesus coaches us to care most of all about the fact that we belong to God for eternity.

When we do, our joy will not be dependent on our success, but rather on the love of God that never lets us go.

Leadership: Seeing the Potential of the Ordinary

If there's one thing that our two consummate coaches have in common, that would be their foresight to opportunity and their view of people's potential. You see, when Belichick came to work as head coach of the New England Patriots, the team did not have an impressive record. The team was an underdog, quite insignificant, and generally unsuccessful. But Belichick had an idea. He saw the potential of the team and its players.

Jesus, too, had a different way of choosing his team of 12 disciples. His selection was considered laughable to many at that time – he chose a group of fishermen, and a tax collector to become his "Disciple Team." These were people who did not even have the gift of public speaking or of writing. His disciples were ordinary people who live day in and out looking for money to feed their families, without concern for their potential or skill, or talent. This group is not from high society. They are without any special skills.

But Jesus saw their potential. He saw their hearts. He saw the willingness of His disciples and He brought them with Him to grow. How effective was it? Well, looking at the Christian religion forming 31% share of the world religions, and the biggest in the world, I should say, the selection was perfect!

Leadership: A Mission of Sacrifice

The time of Jesus was unlike our era where freedom of speech is widely accepted and in fact, encouraged. Jesus and his 12 disciples had to risk spreading the message of Jesus as it is considered something "against tradition" or against religious belief. This led to Jesus being extremely hated and despised by the Pharisees at that time, ultimately causing him to be crucified – all because of His teachings.

But Jesus knew he had to endure and accept His fate. He has predicted His death. He knew that death is part of His mission. In fact, it is His sole mission.

In the Gospel of Mark, generally agreed to be the earliest Gospel, written around the year 70, Jesus predicts His death three times, as recorded in the Bible. In Mark 8:31-33 it says, "He then began to teach them that the Son of Man must suffer many things and be rejected by the elders, the chief priests and the teachers of the law, and that he must be killed and after three days rise again. He spoke plainly about this, and Peter took him aside and began to rebuke him.

But when Jesus turned and looked at his disciples, he rebuked Peter. "Get behind me, Satan!" he said. "You do not have in mind the concerns of God, but merely human concerns."

More verses in the bible, including Mark 9:30-32, and 10:32-34 narrate Jesus' own prediction of His death. Jesus' death is the purpose of the mission, an endgame. It was a final sacrifice and the payment of the debt of sins.

Therefore, it is safe to say that Jesus led a mission that would bring His life to end. Imagine a coach who would train His disciples to do what would cause detriment to His life.

The reason is, Jesus' leadership is not only a *leadership of service,* but also a *leadership of sacrifice.*

Chapter 9

Belichick and Jesus:

The Characteristics of Consummate Coaches

In the first few chapters of this book, we learned that it takes 3Hs to become a consummate coach. We also made parallels of the characteristics of a coach vis-à-vis with water. We also determined the personality of a shepherd and how it relates to a consummate coach's life and ways. Assessing the life of our two consummate coaches – Jesus Christ and Bill Belichick, what makes them the ideal consummate coaches based on our definitions?

There is no denying, Jesus and Belichick used their 3Hs – *Head, Heart, and Hand* – in their quest to achieve their individual goals.

In this chapter, let's make a final assessment of the various characteristics of our consummate coaches in connection to our definition.

Belichick: The Water-Character and The Shepherd

Let's look at Belichick's personality: Belichick does not possess a charismatic personality. Many people often regard him as someone aloof to the public. He avoids the media. He is not a natural speaker. He is a man of few words; but speaks only short yet meaningful words.

In terms of the *polarity and solvency* characteristics (or water's ability to transform into solid, liquid, and gas or the coach's ability to adjust to varying degrees of challenges in your environment), Belichick ultimately takes these characteristics to heart, and it shows in his life.

This characteristic of Belichick is magnified in his ways of doing things, and the meaning behind the words he teaches to his members: On the doorway where the players routinely enter and exit through, there are a few brief printed statements. Some are placed on the side when entering and some on the side when exiting. One quote stands prominent in the team's doorway and says: *"Ignore the Noise."*

I should say that when one knows the skill of ignoring the noise around him, that person is truly one who mastered firmness. He knows that when the world talks, you are firm to disregard it and avoid it as it could distract you. For Belichick, this is the way for his team to not lose themselves, their identity.

Belichick knows that when one starts to listen to the criticism (or even praises) of the world, we lose the capability of possessing those polar and solvent characteristics due to the tendency of some to live their lives and decide things based on the "noise" of the world. Remember that if one has the polar and solvent characteristics, he can jive well with his environment and even those "different elements" around him. But "ignoring the noise" does not mean not listening to it. For Belichick, we still listen but we know when and how to ignore the as we set our eyes on the goal.

This is exactly what water's polar and solvent characteristics are all about. Water acts as a polar solvent because it can be attracted to either the positive or negative electrical charge on a solute, depending on the circumstances. But at the end of the day, regardless of where the water is attracted to, it stays in its identity.

Going back, why is Belichick concerned about the "noise"? When we hear the noise around us – negative or positive - either one becomes demotivated or becomes too proud of himself. Both situations end up with the possibility of losing yourself. Belichick wants his players to never lose their identity. Solvency or Polarity is being able to combine with whatever other elements, and be flexible with the environmental factors. Remember, water will always be water.

Another story speaks volumes of Belichick's heart. Henry Mckenna, AFC East Reporter writes, 'During the season, the Patriots coach holds weekly meetings in his office, including Tuesdays for the starting quarterback and Fridays for the team's captains. Those sessions are blocked out and planned to maximize the conversation for teaching and collaboration. But Belichick doesn't want players to feel like they can't access him outside those meetings. As intimidating as Belichick might seem on the field or in press conferences, players have found that they can walk in and chat with him almost anytime.

About anything.

So I was curious about which players have approached Belichick — and why. Because Belichick really is there for his guys. Obviously, he's always ready to talk football. But he's also there for players who need to discuss marriage, fatherhood, brotherhood, systemic racism, kneeling during the national anthem, and the George Floyd protests."

You see, our consummate coach possesses the character of a good shepherd. He has shown his love and concern for his players and also often portrays himself as a father to them. He also possesses the *capability of reflection* by making sure that his players will see themselves in him by allowing them to freely discuss whatever they feel like discussing. There is real human-to-human interaction, and barriers of communication are torn down, with Belichick displaying a consummate coach quality.

In several instances, Belichick also displayed his fatherly love for his members. When then-offensive coordinator Josh McDaniels lost his father, Belichick gave emphasis on the importance of family.

"He was incredible," McDaniels told FOX Sports. "All he did was make sure that everything was good on our end and if there was anything else I needed from him, 'Let me know what it is.' And, 'Hey, if there's anything the kids need, let me know what that is.' And he wasn't just bulls***ting. That was all real."

Like a shepherd to his flock, Belichick made sure he helps the lost. Indeed a true leader with a heart.

Jesus: Water-Character and Shepherd

Jesus did get all the check marks: he was an *excellent solvent* that adjusted to the varying tribulations of His life. Despite it, He never faltered, rather remained focused. He had the *polarity character* by dining with the sinners and making them stay close to Him despite the judgment from the Pharisees; He is undeniably a *life source*, providing the world the ultimate light against darkness by sharing salvation and the way to Eternity.

But it was not only Jesus' life that we can parallel to a consummate coach. His death, too, displayed the ultimate consummate coach character.

Let me go back to one of the definitions of water solvency: Water's extensive capability to dissolve a variety of molecules has earned it the designation of "universal solvent," and it is this ability that makes water such an invaluable life-sustaining force.

Jesus on the other hand, gave it all. His life, included. By giving His life, it did not mean losing everything or devaluing who He is. He still is Jesus. When He rose again after 3 days after His death, it did make clear justification that He is indeed a "universal solvent", a life-sustaining force, capable of dissolving a variety of forces that came his way.

On a biological level, water's role as a solvent helps cells transport and use substances like oxygen or nutrients. In the same manner, Jesus' death also became a vehicle for sinners like us to be vitalized and reunited with the most important element – God. We should note that before Christ came to life, God is seen as the punisher of the world. The punishment for sin was death. When there was relentless unrighteousness in Sodom and Gomora (Genesis 18-19), fire from the heavens burned the entire city.

The Old Testament records these mass killings. These killings were done because of unrighteousness. We can see below the different biblical references to support that:

1. The Flood - Written in Genesis 6-8
2. The Egyptian firstborn sons during the Passover – Written in Exodus 11-12
3. The Canaanites under Moses and Joshua – Written in Numbers 21:2-3; Deuteronomy 20:17; Joshua 6:17, 21
4. The Amalekites annihilated by Saul – Written in 1 Samuel 15

But when Christ came, it brought a New Testament between God and man. Jesus, the Son of God paid the debt of sin that mankind was supposed to endure. Love was given. Mercy was shown.

If water is not solvent enough, oxygen and nutrients in any life form will not be transported to its different parts where it is necessary; otherwise, death is the way to go for all living things. And if Christ was not a *universal solvent*, death would have been the only option.

But Christ wore the hat of a shepherd. He went His way to earth to find the lost sheep so that we may be guaranteed eternal life. He will find the lost sheep whatever it takes, even if it meant His own life.

Chapter 10

Leadership

As a state representative for years, I have come to know the various leadership or coaching styles and techniques from various literature and experiences from my years of study and exposure to leaders and fellow lawmakers. Working with the government, we often look forward to solving a variety of issues and problems in our state starting from the communities. Revisit old laws and create new ones for the benefit of all.

While we pass and revise laws, implementation is most vital, giving "teeth" to the laws created or revised. Without a doubt, no matter how perfect a law is, that law is without strength without the existence of good leadership. Leadership that promotes honesty, truth, selflessness, and compassion is one that brings changes, and in effect, transforms lives. Leadership is what harmonizes the implementation of laws.

Whether a particular leader is born or made, it is vital for leaders and leader-*wannabes* to have a model of leadership – someone who will mentor and set a good example for them in creating the changes we want to happen around us. When we can breed new good leaders, we are off to become an even stronger nation. Remember, *consummate coaches breed consummate coaches.* In the same manner, *good leaders breed good leaders.*

In this chapter, I want us to look at the leadership characteristics particularly that of Jesus Christ as we make a comparison of His leadership to the standards of world leaders. What makes His leadership different than our own standards of leadership?

Jesus: A Standout Leader

Every leader has a model leader. A leader copies his style of leadership to that model. Leadership styles, techniques, and methods are often duplicated. There are no new leadership styles. It is only enhanced every time it is passed on but the core remains the same. The important thing for us is, as leadership styles are passed on from one generation to another, it is important to have good mentors or best examples of leaders today – and I mean in this generation – because the leaders after our generation will soon be looking back at our leadership styles and copy them.

So, what then should the current leaders do? We must look at the best practices of the leaders of the past, and we are off to a good start.

We don't have to go too far! Let's look at our consummate coach's leadership – Jesus Christ's. Katie Taylor wrote this in the World Vision online platform about what makes Jesus' leadership different than politicians and I adopted them here:

We can look to Jesus for examples of wise, loving leadership. But Jesus is so different from many earthly leaders that it seems foolish to compare them — especially when the more important comparison is between Jesus and ourselves. Are *we* speaking the truth? Giving Jesus our whole hearts? Valuing others? Acting with compassion and forgiving much more often than we'd like?

None of us is getting it all right. But election season offers us lots of opportunities for practice! We can speak the truth in love and value the people labeled worthless, who treat us poorly, and even people who disagree with us. We can let our compassion, instead of our desire to be right, motivate our actions. We can forgive, even before being asked. We can be like the leaders we want to see.

Because no matter who gets elected, what will matter most is who we allow to rule our hearts. In that race, we definitely recommend signing up with Jesus.

Here are six ways Jesus is different from the leaders of today, and what those differences teach us.

1. Jesus always speaks the truth.

Remember when Jesus calls the Pharisees a "brood of vipers" (Matthew 12:34)? Ouch. Harsh words. The Pharisees had great religious influence — wouldn't it have been a better strategy to tone it down a bit? But Jesus speaks the truth without fear of repercussions. He's concerned with sharing his message, not gaining political support.

Nor is Jesus using hard-hitting truths as a way to rile up anger from people already on his side. He's not going for the "gotcha" moment or the "truth bomb." Whether or not it's to his advantage, and even if it means he'll lose supporters, he speaks the truth. Because the truth — undiluted — is what sets us free.

Let's pray that our current and future leaders have the strength to speak the truth with love, even when it might be costly.

2. Jesus asks for more and offers more.

We all like easy, and people who seek power often base their campaigns around making things easier for us. "Vote for me: Your concerns will be addressed and your problems solved!" Even if we know in our hearts that it can't be quite that simple, easy can be an attractive offer.

But while Jesus says that his yoke is easy and his burden light (Matthew 11:30), His plan has a steep joining fee. He says, "Whoever wants to be my disciple must deny themselves and take up their cross and follow me" (Matthew 16:24).

"Take up your cross" would be a horrible campaign slogan. No one would go for it. But Jesus is playing the long game; he's playing for eternity. The reward is great though the journey may be rough. But he reminds us it's worth it: "What good is it for someone to gain the whole world, and yet lose or forfeit their very self?" (Luke 9:25). Jesus offers us an eternity full of joy with him, but not in exchange for a vote or a certain percentage of our hearts. He wants more than that — he wants our whole hearts, souls, minds, and strength.

May our commitment to Jesus be far greater than our commitment to earthly leaders, even when following him is difficult.

3. Jesus values us more.

Why is Jesus willing to tell us to deny ourselves and follow him? Because he loves us, and that's what it will take to have a relationship with him. Unlike a political candidate, Jesus doesn't need our support; He wants our company. He wants to enjoy life with us starting here on Earth and continuing into eternity. This is not an offer our earthly leaders can match.

Jesus values us so much that he paid our debt of sin with His death. Paul tells us that, "For the joy set before him he endured the cross, scorning its shame ..." (Hebrews 12:2). The joy of fellowship with us was greater to him than the pain of the cross.

And He doesn't stop there! He's still seeking us, still calling us. He can't be stopped, because His love for us is relentless.

In the election season, we can remember Jesus' great love for humanity and let that guide and direct our interactions with each other.

4. Jesus values all of us.

We've probably all experienced the type of leader that seeks to surround themselves with influential people, hoping (not unwisely) that some of that influence will rub off on them. If you're looking to have an influence on Earth, hanging out with the smart, the beautiful, and the rich is a good strategy.

But it's not how Jesus operates. He not only spends time with people the world rejects but also goes looking for them. He seeks out the ostracized, poor, sick, weak, and people deemed "worthless" — these are the folks Jesus wants to spend time with.

The story of Zacchaeus is a beautiful example of this (Luke 19). Zacchaeus is a despised tax collector working for the Roman government, a cheater, and a sinner. Because he's not tall enough to see over the crowds, Zacchaeus had to climb a tree just to catch a glimpse of Jesus. If anyone else noticed Zacchaeus at all, they would have expected Jesus to walk on by.

But Jesus calls Zacchaeus by name. He sees Zacchaeus in the tree and says that he wants to hang out with him. Zacchaeus' life changes from that moment — he repents of his sin and promises to share his wealth. That's the power of being valued by Jesus.

As always, we pray and advocate that our leaders would remember the most vulnerable among us — the poor, the sick, the refugees — and seek ways to empower them. *Ask your leaders to remember vulnerable children.*

5. Jesus is motivated by compassion.

Our leaders can create amazing change when they allow compassion to motivate them to action. Most of us can understand what it's like to be compelled to act by compassion: We see people hurting, and we want to help.

But Jesus is the compassion champion. He lets compassion mess up his plans, frustrate his followers, and throw his work-life balance out of whack.

We see this clearly right after John the Baptist's death. Jesus withdraws to a remote area to be alone (Matthew 14:13). So often surrounded by crowds, Jesus wanted to be alone after the death of someone important to him. But the crowds of people heard about where he was going, and rather than giving him some space, they followed him and pressed in around him, eager to have their own needs filled.

When we're already tired or sad, the last thing we want is to be confronted by other people's demands, and we often react harshly. But Jesus looked out at the crowds and "had compassion on them and healed their sick" (Matthew 14:14). He set his own needs aside to minister to others, not because he had too, but because his compassion made him want to.

6. Jesus forgives.

Sadly, forgiveness is not always advantageous to our leaders. Think of debate stages where we see candidates reminded of every time they made a mistake, misspoke, or cast an unpopular vote. One candidate brings up their opponent's mistake and vice versa, and it seems whoever memorized the longer list of sins will win the day. Mistakes are used to condemn and destroy.

We need to hold our leaders accountable, but true repentance should be met with true forgiveness. That kind of forgiveness sets us free to be the people God created us to be.

In the book of Matthew, we see Peter trying to be generous by asking Jesus if he should forgive someone "up to seven times" (Matthew 18:21). Jesus shocks him by replying that he shouldn't forgive seven times, but "seventy times seven" (Matthew 18:22). Basically, however much we think we should forgive, we should forgive more.

Jesus doesn't forgive to "be nice" or because it's the socially acceptable thing to do, he forgives to set people free. He doesn't want anything blocking people from living life in all its fullness (John 10:10).

May we value leaders who are willing to forgive, and may we forgive them and not hold grudges that grow bitterness.

Jesus has set a perfect roadmap for leaders and coaches to follow. His life left us with an image of a consummate leader – a compassionate and forgiving leader that values every member of his pack. It is the leadership that exemplified what the very core of humanity is – love. This kind of leadership anchored on love is what Jesus also wants us to live by. In our every day, Jesus wants us to spread His teachings of love to everyone we come in contact with. When we learn to walk in these characteristics, we are off to becoming consummate leaders or individuals ourselves.

Remember, *consummate coaches breed consummate coaches.*

Chapter 11

So What?

Now that we have discussed the lives of our two consummate coaches, let's see how their lives can impact our own.

The first one lives in the present, gained influence and fame through small beginnings, and became an icon of sports, yet stood amidst fame and fortune with humility and respect for people. The other One was born more than 2000 years ago and created a model of leadership for the world to see. Born from poverty but rose to fame and Lordship.

One is named the greatest coach of all time. The other is named the most influential person who ever walked this earth and founded the biggest religion on the planet.

There is indeed much to talk about these two personalities. But one thing stands true today: their lives defined what a consummate coach really is. Both used their *Head, Heart, and Hand in* the process, both possessed the valuable characteristics of water, and both held well their role as the shepherd to their flock.

This book has dived deep into each of our coaches. But what now? One may say, "I can't be a consummate coach anyway". "I am not as gifted, I am not called for service." "I am not chosen." "I simply can't be a leader." "I am not born for big things." How will the consummate coach's life make sense to me?

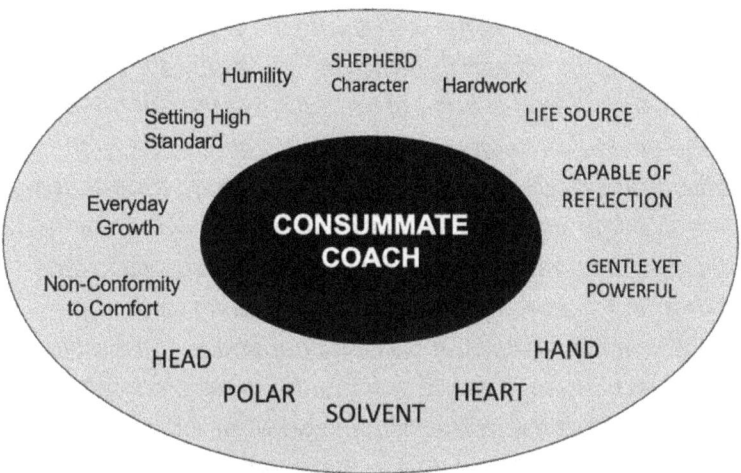

Well, it is true that coaching and leadership are exclusively for a selected few in our society. Not everyone who walks on the face of this planet will become a coach or a leader – more so a consummate coach. Only chosen ones will take on huge responsibilities. Thus, a big percentage of our population will be dependent on the *teaching, training, and decision-making skills* of coaches and leaders. Our own world, in fact, is currently shaped by our leaders' decisions - our bosses, our political officials, and our community leaders. The fate of your world rests upon a selected group of people.

But the good news is, when we personify the consummate coach characteristics in our lives, it only takes only one life to be inspired and be touched and we shall leave a mark that can possibly change not just someone's life, but the fate of the whole world.

Like how Belichick sees the potential of others, we need to practice the mentality of seeing the potential of others – the potential of the younger people around us. They, too, might become leaders of their generation. Teaching them the values we discussed today could impact the world in the future.

Personify the Consummate Coach in Your Soul

In my other book *"Extreme Entrepreneurs: Steve Jobs and Jesus Christ"* I spoke about the definition and importance of our soul:

"The intangible that makes us who we are as people, animals, or plants. It is the force that moves us to action, the arbiter of emotions, the source of inspiration, the hesitation or bounce in our step, the scale that keeps us in balance, and the voice that keeps us motivated or not. According to John Ortberg in Soul Keeping, your soul is your "youness." Richard Rohr, in Falling Upward, says, "Your soul has many secrets. They are only revealed to those who want them and are never completely forced on us."

In this definition, we can say that our soul is the director of our lives. It directs us to what we want to do, gives us an idea of what we ought to do, and challenges us to do what is right. It is the core of our persona. It is connected to our mind.

In fact, our minds are interlinked to the soul because what the mind thinks, the soul perceives. In the earlier chapters, I shared the quote, *"The mind is the theater of the soul".* Thus, when we personify the characteristics of our consummate coaches, it should not only come from the heart. We think like them. When we do so, we go deep within our souls and our persona, and match it to the characteristics of our consummate coaches.

Imagine living our lives patterned after our consummate coaches, Jesus and Belichick. We can emulate their ways and put them in our own. We can use their strategies and leadership styles and apply them in our households, in our offices, and in our interactions with our fellow employees, our neighbors, or colleagues.

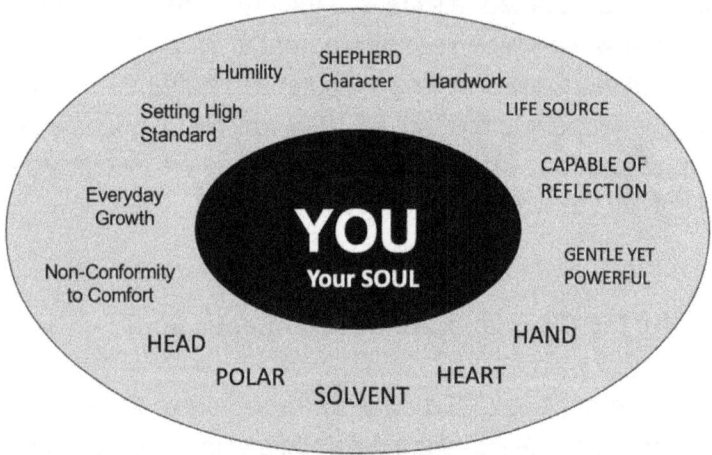

Looking at the figure above, we set our soul in the middle because our soul will drive us to action. When we surround ourselves with the characteristics of our consummate coaches, live them, and put them into our hearts, we gain the ability to personify the individuals we studied.

Hardwork and perseverance are values we need to strive to achieve everyday. When we reach our individual success, we practice *humility*. We aim for *everyday growth*, we set a *high standard,* and we *do not conform to our comfort zone.*

Like water, we are *valuable, but we are not expensive.* We are overflowing and we are willing to share our own skills with others because we have the ability of *solvency*, of *polarity*, and we are a *life source*. Like Jesus we are willing to lend a hand to anyone who needs our help because personify *gentleness*. But we can be *powerful* too. When we are oppressed, we fight and stand for truth. We continually gather our knowledge for the enhancement of our skills to sharpen our *Head*, and we also put them to good use by practical uses through our *Hand*. Our hands constantly bring good fruits and are always willing to extend them to those who need us and give back to those who paved opportunities for us.

In everything that we do, we fuel ourselves with our *Heart* – compassion, love, concern for the needy, the will to survive; the passion for success; the achievement of our life goals. When we do so, we can become our own consummate coach. Let us personify our consummate coaches.

Slowly, we build our own *consummate life* out of the skills and characteristics of our *consummate coach*. This will be reflected outwardly so that people around us will feel and see its light. Then you multiply.

Be like Bill Belichick. Be Christ-like.